Options Trading for a Living

Make a Passive Income from Home with the Best Techniques and Advanced Strategies Investing in the Stock Market (Crash Course for Beginners 2021).

Pat Cross

TABLE OF CONTENTS

INTRODUCTION..2

OPTIONS TRADING FOR A LIVING......................7

METHODS FOR ANALYSING MARKET...............36

COMMON MISTAKES TO AVOID..................…...45

WHAT IS THE STOCK MARKET?...........................53

HOW TO MAKE MONEY IN THE STOCK MARKET FOR BEGINNERS STEP BY STEP PLAN............…65

HOW TO GO PUBLIC WITH LITTLE MONEY

DAY TRADING STRATEGIES FOR BEGINNERS

RULES FOR SUCCESSFUL TRADING

CONCLUSION..85

INTRODUCTION

To win in circulation, you must outperform the masses of competitors. You must lose the majority to be able to pay whoever wins. To become a successful trader, you must beat the odds against you. You must learn to think and act differently from the crowd in the market. The new business for a living contains many unconventional business ideas. The goal of this introduction is to pause at the beginning of your journey and see if it supports some of the less conventional ideas about trading.

Why are these options misinterpreted as a minefield full of dangers? How can we understand this and see opportunities as tools to reduce our risks, increase our returns, and learn what we are doing simultaneously? That's How to Simplify Complex Things Seemingly. Options have become remarkably popular, especially in the US. Far from being restricted to just institutions and professional money managers, options trading is now common for retail traders from all walks of life.

The most significant risk in trading comes from the person reading this book: your emotions often tip the balance between winning and losing. If you can stay calm and make rational decisions, you will keep track of your trading profits. The professional trader is calm and profitable.

You know what to do if the market goes up, down, or diverges—patiently watching the market from the sidelines. If you get giddy with joy as the market goes on its way but freeze in fear when it swings against you, your actions will be emotional, and your account will suffer. When the mind is clouded by greed or fear, the best trading systems fly out.

Can you make a living with options trading? One of the first things to consider is whether trading is the way you want to spend your life. Negotiating livelihood options is essentially a job and not necessarily a profession for everyone. Imagine that you are interviewing for this job and interviewing yourself. Be very honest and answer the following questions

How long do you need to develop your skills? Trading is a complex skill that requires practice, and you will not be able to live off your trading income until your skills are exceptional, and you can apply them consistently over the months. How ready are you to study and learn? There are many technical aspects of the options, so you need the right mindset, motivation to study, and readiness for complex technical concepts. If it is fun for you, as it is for me, it can be both fun and intellectually beneficial.

Do you have a personality that suits options trading? You need the right mood to be a successful trader. What is your risk tolerance? Or in other words, where are you in your life? How old are you, and how much can you lose and still be fine? You will inevitably face losses along the way; Can you physically survive those periods? Where do you see yourself in the next five years?

However, the concept of options is still treated with fear and apprehension in some quarters. When I first embarked on a serious trade, a friend warned me about what he was doing, but the trade can be as safe as you like. The simple fact is, you need a successful business plan. You need to keep your risks low and the chance of your reward high. You need your plan to be structured and straightforward so that you can follow it at all times. Over the years, my business plan has become progressively simpler. To make you a merchant, the following traits are worth developing, and they can all be developed.

Criteria For A Successful Investing

- Patience

- Perseverance

- Knowledge

- Honesty

- Advance Planning

- Patience Discipline

OPTIONS TRADING FOR A LIVING

Trading stock options can be complicated and even more complicated than trading stocks. When you buy a stock, you simply decide how many shares you want, and your broker executes the order at the prevailing market price or the exact price you set. Options trading requires an understanding of advanced strategies, and the process of opening an options trading account includes a few more steps than opening a typical investment account. Learn more about the differences between stocks and options.

Examples and strategies of option is a contract that allows (but does not require) an investor to buy or sell an underlying instrument such as security, ETF, or index at a specified price for a specified period. But what is options trading? If you haven't noticed this yet, there are a lot of options when it comes to investing in securities. Whether you prefer playing the stock market or investing in an ETF or two, you probably know the basics of various stocks. But what exactly are options, and what is options trading?

What Are The Options?

An option is a contract that allows (but does not require) an investor to buy or sell an underlying instrument such as a stock, ETF, or even an index at a predetermined price for a certain period. Buy and sell options are made on the options market, which trades contracts based on securities. Buying an option that allows you to purchase shares at a later time is called a "call option," while buying an option that will enable you to sell shares at a later time is called a "put option."

However, options are not the same as stocks, as they do not represent ownership of the company. Although futures contracts are used as options, chances are considered to be less risky because you can withdraw (or walk away from) an options contract at any time. Therefore, the option price (in addition to this) is a percentage of the underlying asset or security.

When buying or selling options, the investor or trader has the right to exercise that option at any time until the expiration date, so buying or selling an option does not mean that you have to exercise it at the point of purchase/sale. Because of this system, options are considered derivative securities, which means that their price is derived from something else (in this case, the value of an asset such as the market, stocks, or another underlying instrument). For this reason, options are often considered less risky than stocks (if used correctly).

But why does an investor use option? Well, put options are betting that stocks go up or down or cover a position in the market. The price at which you agree to buy the underlying security through the option is called the "strike price," and the fee you pay to buy the option contract is called the "premium." By determining the strike price, you bet that the asset (usually a stock) will go up or down in price. The price you pay for this bet is the premium, which is a percentage of the value of that asset.

Some Basic Terms That You Should Know

When you learn to trade options, you will come across the same conditions that you need to know:

Call options - give you the right, but not the obligation, to purchase the underlying security at a specified price on a specified day.

Put options - give you the right, but not the obligation, to sell an asset at a specified price on a specific day.

Strike Price - The strike price is the exact price you will buy or sell the underlying shares.

Contract Expiration - This is the day when the options contract expires, and the trader can exercise their right to buy or sell shares.

Insurance Premiums- Option premiums are the price paid by the buyer of the option contract to sell the contract. These are priced per share.

There are two different types of options,

- Call options
- Put options

which gives the investor the right (but not the obligation) to sell or buy securities.

Purchase Options

A call option is a contract that gives an investor the right to buy a certain number of shares (usually 100 per contract) of a specific security or commodity at a particular price within a specified period. For example, the call option will allow the trader to buy a certain number of stocks, be it stocks, bonds, or even other instruments like ETFs or indices, later (at the expiration of the contract period).

If you are buying a put option, this means that you want the share price (or any other value) to go up so that you can make a profit on your contract by exercising your right to buy those shares, and you usually sell immediately to take advantage of the profit.

The fee you pay to buy a call option is called a premium (it is the purchasing cost of the contract that will ultimately allow you to buy the stock or security). In this sense, the premium for a call option is like a down payment, as you could put it on a house or a car. When buying a call option, you agree with the seller on the strike price and are given the option to buy the security at a predetermined price (which does not change until the contract expires).

Call options are a lot like insurance: you pay for a contract that expires at a specific time but allows you to buy a security (such as shares) at a predetermined price (which will not increase even if it is a stock. in the market). market). However, you will have to renew your option (usually weekly, monthly, or quarterly). For this reason, options always face what is called time reduction, which means that their value decreases over time. For call options, the lower the strike price, the greater the intrinsic value of the call option.

Selling Options

Instead, a put option is a contract that gives the investor the right to sell a certain number of shares (again, usually 100 per contract) of a particular security or commodity at a specified price for a specified period. Like a call option, a put option gives a trader the right (but not the obligation) to sell a security before the contract expires.

Like call options, the price you agree to sell the stock is called the strike price, and the premium is the fee you pay for the put option. Put options work in a similar way to put options, except that you want the security value to decrease if you buy a put option for profit (or sell the put option if you think the price will rise). Unlike call options, with put options, the higher the strike price, the greater the intrinsic value of the call option.

Long Or Short Option

Unlike other securities such as futures contracts, options trading is usually "long," which means that you are buying the option hoping that the price will rise (in this case, you would buy a call option). However, even if you have purchased a put option (the right to sell the security), you are still buying a put option.

Selling an option means selling that option, but the proceeds from the sale are limited to the premium of the option, and the risk is unlimited. The more time remaining in the contract, the higher the premiums for both buy and sell options.

Beginning Options Trading

Making money from Options trading is a magnet for people looking to make a living from trading. Whether that means full-time or supplemental income, the idea of doing it from home in as little as a few hours a day is exciting.

But is it realistic to negotiate income options for a living? Yes, the most significant part of the options market is that it is very flexible, as there are many ways to deal with it. Options trading can be a great way to make money, but it isn't easy to read options trading books before trading to make sure you know what you are doing.

How To Become A Professional Options Trader

Getting involved in the options market is not a complex process. Of course, you have to find a broker online and have the funds available to trade, but you can decide how to become an options trader in three different areas:

- Look for an options trading system that provides obvious entry and exit points.

- One of the biggest mistakes traders makes is entering a trade without a plan. Without a roadmap to follow, the emotional side of trading can make mistakes.

- No guessing when to get in and out. Everything we are decided for you. With a system that puts the odds in your favor, you can trade with confidence.

Benefits of options trading

The benefits of options trading are many:

- Great leverage when trading options
- Minimum time required to operate
- Profit in many different market countries

- The risk is limited

Leverage - You can take advantage of the significant leverage when trading with your online broker. As retailers, you only have access to limited funds, so you need to make sure you are using that money well, and leverage is one way you can use it to do this.

Options allow us to take control of suitably sized positions for as little as a few hundred dollars. Imagine that you control a hundred shares of Google for a fraction of the cost of owning the shares.

Minimum time: unlike day traders, you don't sit in front of your screen and see all the flashing quotes. You can view your charts once a day and determine if there are any options trading settings. This is ideal for someone busy with another job, family obligations, or even enjoying retirement.

Trading for a living does not necessarily mean living for trading. This is one of the significant drawbacks to day trading but one of the many benefits of options trading.

Profit in many market conditions - Options are the only tool available that allows you to profit from markets that are moving up, down, or sideways. This is powerful because it will enable you to make a profit regardless of what the market does. This is very important for a trader looking to live from the markets and trade full time.

Limited Risk - Your risk is limited by the cost of the option. You can set up strategies in which the risk of loss is minimized, but the trading potential is very high. Every trader will tell you that preservation of capital is the number one task of any trader.

You can earn money from premiums if you are an option seller. Many professional options traders who make a living trading these markets do so by selling bank options.

Find Markets That Suit Your Trading Style.

Another big mistake that traders make is trading many markets that they were not familiar with. The best part of trading options for a living is that it allows you to trade some high-flying stocks like Apple and Google.

Most successful traders trade the same stocks and ETFs every day, which allows them to trade full time with confidence. No stock survey needs to be done daily. Trading under the same list of names allows the trader to know how these products are moving.

If you are looking for higher frequencies, consider more tech names like Apple and Netflix. If you are looking for fewer repetitions, you can always focus on ETFs that allow you to familiarize yourself with a whole basket of stocks.

Diversification For Option Trading

People often avoid seeing the stock market as a source of income because they believe there is a high failure rate. Like any other business, there will be people who will strive to be successful. One of the reasons for this is that they take a lot of risks.

Regardless of the size of your account, you must ensure that you use the correct risks in your operations. This means making sure your account is spread across different products rather than putting all your money in one or two hubs. Any options trading success story you read will tell you that managing your risk is one of the most important things you can do as a trader.

The greater your ability to diversify, the smoother your equity curve will be. Trading options allow you to diversify better than most other products out there. You can trade more instruments due to the leverage it provides.

When considering diversification, also consider whether you should trade weekly or monthly options. This will simply add to your business inventory, and you won't have all of your eggs in one basket. You can also use different trading strategies to take advantage of different market conditions and trade full time for a living.

How Much Money Do You Need To Live?

You cannot decide if you can earn a living from a job without understanding your financial situation. If you are young, single, and have relatively few large expenditures, you might be able to live on $ 2,000 a month. On the other hand, if you have a family, kids, mortgage, and school loans and your monthly expenses will be higher, your monthly income requirements will be higher.

Your first step before making a big financial decision is assessing your money. Calculate the minimum amount you need to bring each month to cover all necessary expenses, plus additions like saving some money, going out to eat, going to a show, dating, or whatever else you want to do.

You may choose to forgo some of these additions at first, but eventually, you'll want a balance in your life. The pursuit of profit should not be at the expense of living your life.

How Much Capital Do You Have?

This is the most important factor whether you can do it full time or just a hobby or side activity. If you do not have capital, you must move to another company. The saying that "making money takes money" is quite proper for options trading. To get started, you need startup capital. Some of them should be in cash, but ideally, you should also own stocks as long-term investments.

Potential Income On A Capital Basis

You cannot earn a lot if your capital is small. Even with an account of $ 100,000, you'll only make about $ 25,000 a year, which isn't enough for most people to live. The higher your equity, the more difficult it will be to reach your profit target, as you must have more or more active positions at the same time. Expanding is challenging, so expect diminishing returns as your account grows.

It is incredibly challenging to achieve consistent returns week after week. The market itself is inconsistent. It's easy to slip into a false sense of competition in a long-lasting bull market, especially if you don't know anything else. Prepare yourself mentally and financially for bad times, as it is an integral part of trading. 0.5% per week doesn't sound like a lot, but in simple terms, it equates to about 25% per year.

Most hedge fund managers and professional traders will be thrilled with 25% annual returns, which means it is tough to achieve. Could your strange weekly earnings be higher? Sure, but it could also be less—a conservative plan.

The flip side of the previous point is that it is somewhat easier for an individual retail trader to achieve higher returns than an institutional trader who trades with much more significant amounts, more demands on their performance, and tighter restrictions on risk management.

Can You Do That?

As you can see, it is possible to earn enough by trading options, but only if you have meager living expenses (that is, you are young and single) or have a large amount of capital to use. Either way, this is my advice, based on how you do it:

Why Do You Also Own Stocks?

You want to own stocks in the long term because this is how you build steady long-term wealth. If you live on the money you make from options, by definition, the money does not add to your net worth as much as you spend some or all of your living expenses. Stocks also provide financial stability. You're not likely to risk your long-term holdings by monetizing them to buy options, as they provide some kind of baseline for your portfolio.

At night, you think you don't want to restrict all of your money to Long Term Buy and Hold (LTBH) stocks, but it's not as bad as you might think. You can leverage your LTBH investment through your buying power (BP) in your margin account. Purchasing power is the amount that you can spend on a given day on trading-related activities in your account. It is the sum of your cash balance plus your available margin, which is the amount that you can borrow for commercial purposes.

Obtaining and using a margin loan is a poor and risky decision, but purchasing power is a powerful tool in your options traders. Think of BP as an alternative currency available to you. Your LTBH investment contributes to your BP even if it is not actual cash in your account. Keep in mind that you must manage your PA carefully and not misuse it as part of your risk management strategy.

So, do your research, do your due diligence, and then buy stocks from quality companies that you want to keep for years, if not decades. Use it as a base for growth and leverage your capital to support options trading.

Regardless of the equity, how much capital you need depends on the return on that capital. A reasonable goal might be 1% weekly, but you won't achieve your goal every week of every year. Being more conservative, let's say you average a return of 0.5% per week for 50 weeks per year.

Don't quit your day job if you have one.

Start learning about investments and options. There are many free resources online, including the Options Hive, that you can use to start an organization. Read and learn everything you can from trusted sources before risking real money.

Choose the options trading strategy that makes the most sense to you and matches your personality traits. However, I have my preferences and ideas on how to become a successful retail options trader. There are many different ways to trade, and your opinions will be gained through reading, learning, and experience. Swap the paper for a while until you are entirely comfortable with the mechanics and are confident that your technique will consistently generate income.

Get started very slowly with genuine financial transactions. Be patient. Make a contract or two and let them play. Learn to handle good situations as well as the inevitable bad situations that conflict with you. If you're not patient, they shouldn't be business options that, by definition, take time to work. I didn't achieve much in the first two years after I started trading options, but I did learn a lot.

When you find what works for you, start increasing your trading volume and number of positions. At the same time, keep investing some of your money in LTBH stocks to increase your long-term net worth. Find the right balance between the two for yourself.

Day Trading Options Right For You?

Over the years, traders have added day trading options along with their other market tactics. With the ability to take advantage of high-priced and effective stocks for little money, trading options daily is a viable way to benefit from this market.

But is this approach right for you?

As with all approaches to trading, day trading options have advantages and disadvantages that every trader interested in options trading should be aware of.

Day Trading Options: Advantage

- Large leverage allows you to gain control over expensive stocks for a fraction of the cost
- Weekly options trading can lead to huge moves quickly. Options interact faster
- For changes in the share price as the maturity date approaches.
- A fast trade can pay off big, especially when trading at the end of the day

Day Trading Options - The Downside

You never know when big moves will happen. To see consistent results, you need to be on the charts throughout the day; day trading futures can be much easier, as activities usually occur at more predictable times.

You need to check out a more extensive watchlist for stocks and ETFs because you don't know which names will be active that day. This requires more preparatory work daily. If the trade takes too long, downtime and volatility may lead to larger losses. Before considering risking your trading capital on day options, be sure to find an acceptable downside. If not, there are other ways to take advantage of the options market's diversity.

Do Options Traders Make Money?

The answer, it depends. From YOU to get what you want and how to prepare to trade for a living, you have to have tons of variables (like the ones we talked about earlier) online. One of the things we're talking about is logging all of your trades to make sure you don't slowly bleed out of your account. Using an options trading spreadsheet to ensure that you record your transactions is a step you must take to ensure that your trading feature remains valid.

Some would say $ 275 is not much to live in, and it's true. This represents exchange. Options traders generally have multiple trades in operation, and since you can make money in any market situation, I believe you can see the potential. Trading is a profession, and the better prepared you are, the better your chances of success.

Livelihood Options Are 100% Possible

It is possible, my friends. It is. Don't be fooled by any "expert" who promises to alert you to profitable trade setups or other such follies. Keep it simple. You have an adequate amount of working capital and 2-3 years of living expenses in the bank, and I promise you that it is possible to get some bargains with reasonable returns by selling options.

Learn about all options trading strategies, control your risks and diversify your prominent positions. Another essential thing to keep in mind is that you should keep your rates as low as possible. Don't overpay commissions because every dollar you spend to make a deal is one dollar withdrawn from your account.

METHODS FOR ANALYSING MARKET

Fundamental Analysis

Fundamental analysis is the study of individual companies and their performance in terms of

- income-earning

- assets

- loans

In simple terms, most of the significant financial indices you will see are juggling these four elements. Why do we need to know fundamental analysis? Because the price of a company's stock is ultimately the market's reflection of how valuable that company is. Suppose the company is making a profit, and those profits are growing year over year, with loans at low levels and also increasing income. In that case, this is an ideal company to invest in, as long as you expect the company to continue to grow at these levels.

Remember that expectations primarily drive stock prices. Expectations are fueled by current sentiment. Sentiments are mainly influenced by news and history. The corporate information includes the company's financial results and its plans for the future. In a broader perspective, the news covers the economy in general, both nationally and internationally.

Technical Analysis

What is technical analysis? It's graph reading. More specifically, it is the science (or art) of recognizing and interpreting chart patterns to make time-related buy and sell decisions and implement a business plan. Technical analysis can help you make your decisions and make them more accurate, make them more disciplined, and help you manage your money more effectively.

Many supporters of technical analysis believe that everything you need to know about safety can be seen on the charts. The technical analysis comes in two forms:

- **Price patterns**: These are simply visual patterns of what is happening to the price of a security.

- **Indicators**: They are mathematical algorithms that take all aspects of price movement, including volume, and combine to form all kinds of relationships and analyses through which price movement can be estimated in the future.

PRICE PATTERNS

Three ways to look at price patterns are simply the patterns of price movements of a security over a known time scale.

There are three main ways to display price movement during any period:

- Uptrend movement
- Downtrend movement
- Consolidation movement

Support And Resistance

Support and Resistance Most traders and investors use support and resistance. At its simplest, it is the most straightforward pattern that can be understood and the easiest to recognize just by looking at the graphs.

- Support is where price finds a base (floor) from which it bounces up.

- Resistance is where the price meets a peak from which it bounces down. Where previous lows and highs have formed clear support and resistance lines, the psychology of these levels plays a role.

Traders may be wary of the resistance level and sell while becoming more enthusiastic when the stock reaches its support level. If the action exceeds these levels, then you will play other tactics. Nobody knows for sure when the support or resistance will hold or break, and we don't want to delve into expectations anyway.

The best way to trade support and resistance is to place conditional orders if they break out in a continuation context, as the trend continues. Often when the support and resistance lines are broken, they form the opposite of what they were before, i.e., the old support becomes the new resistance, and the old resistance becomes the new support.

Options Trading Strategies: A Beginner's Guide

Options are conditional derivative contracts that allow contract buyers (option holders) to buy or sell a security at a chosen price. Option buyers bear an amount called a "premium" by sellers for this right.

If market prices are unfavorable for option holders, they will let the option expire worthless, thus ensuring that the losses do not exceed the premium. In contrast, option sellers (option book) take more risk than option buyers, thus claiming this premium.

The options are divided into "call" and "sell" options. With a call option, the buyer of the contract buys the right to buy the underlying asset in the future at a predetermined price, called the strike price or strike price. With a put option, the buyer acquires the right to sell the underlying asset in the future at the predetermined price.

Call purchase (long calls) This is the preferred strategy for traders who are "bullish" or confident in a particular stock, ETF, or index and want to limit risk. You want to take advantage of leverage to take advantage of higher prices

Options are leveraged instruments; that is, they allow traders to increase interest by risking lower amounts than would be required if the underlying asset were traded. A standard stock option contract controls 100 shares of the underlying stock.

Suppose a trader wants to invest $ 5,000 in Apple (AAPL) and is trading around $ 165 per share. With this amount, he can buy 30 shares for $ 4,950. Let's say, then, that the stock price rises 10% to $ 181.50 over the next month. Ignoring any brokerage, commission, or transaction fees, the merchant's portfolio would amount to $ 5,445, leaving the merchant with a net dollar return of $ 495, or 10% of the invested capital.

Now, let's say a stock option at a strike price of $ 165 that expires in about a month costs $ 5.50 a share or $ 550 per contract. Given the investment budget available to a trader, he can purchase nine options for $ 4,950. Since the option contract controls 100 shares, the trader makes an effective trade with 900 shares.

If the share price increases 10% to $ 181.50 at expiration, the option will expire in the money and be valued at $ 16.50 per share ($ 181.50 - $ 165 for strike), or $ 14,850 for 900 shares. This is a net dollar return of $ 9,990, or 200% on invested capital, which is a much higher return than the direct trading of the underlying asset. For related reading, see Should an investor hold or exercise an option?

Risk / Reward: The potential operator loss from a prolonged call is limited to the premium paid. The potential profit is unlimited, as the payment of the option will increase with the price of the underlying asset until expiration. Theoretically, there is no limit to how high it will be.

COMMON MISTAKES TO AVOID

One of the common mistakes traders make is that they believe they should stick to a call or put option until the expiration date. Suppose the underlying stock of your option rises overnight (doubling the value of the call or put option). In that case, you can immediately exercise the contract to make a profit (even if you have, say, 29 days for the option).

Another common mistake of options traders (especially beginners) is not creating a good exit plan for your option. For example, you may want to plan to exit your choice when you incur a loss or when you make a profit that satisfies you (rather than continuing your contract until the expiration date).

However, other traders may make the mistake of thinking that the cheaper, the better. As for the options, this is not necessarily true. The more affordable the option, the more "no money" the option, which can be a riskier investment with less profit potential if it goes wrong. Buying call or put options "out of the money" means you want the underlying security to change in value, which is not always predictable drastically.

And while there are many other wrong options, be sure to do your research before getting into the options trading game.

How To Trade Options In 4 Steps

Trading stock options requires answering these questions: In what direction will stock move, how far will they go, and when will they happen?

1. Open an options trading account

Before you start trading options, you will need to show that you know what you are doing. (Need to speed up the order, sell, strike price, and other trading options? Compared to opening a brokerage account for trading stocks, opening an options trading account requires more significant amounts of capital. Given the complexity of forecasting the many moving parts, brokers should learn more about a potential investor before they are permitted to start trading options.

Brokerage firms select potential options traders to assess their trading experience, understand risks and financial preparedness. These details will be documented in the options trading agreement used to obtain approval from your potential broker. You will need to provide the following: Investment goals. This generally includes income, growth, capital maintenance, or speculation.

Business experience. The broker will want to know your investing knowledge, how long you trade stocks or options, the number of trades you make per year, and the volume of your trades—personal financial information. Have your net worth (or easily sold investments for cash), annual income, total net worth, and employment information close at hand.

The types of options you want to trade. For example, calls, status, or spread. And if it is covered or bare. The seller or issuer of the options is obligated to deliver the underlying shares if the option is executed. If the subscriber also owns the underlying equity, the option position is hedged. If the option position is left unprotected, it is empty.

2. Choose options to buy or sell

To remember, a call option is a contract that gives you the right, but not the obligation, to buy a share at a predetermined price (called the strike price) for a certain period. A put option gives you the right, but not the obligation, to sell shares at a specified price before the contract expires.

Depending on the direction you expect the underlying stock to move, determine the type of options contract to take; if you think the share price will go up: buy a put or call option. If you think the stock price will remain constant: sell a put option or a put option. If you think the share price will go down: buy a put option or a put option

3. Predict the option strike price

When an option is purchased, it remains valuable only if the share price closes the expiration date of the option "in the money." This means above or below the strike price. (For call options, the price is higher than the exercise; for call options, it is lower than the exercise.) You will need to buy a chance with a strike price that reflects where you expect the stock to be during the life of the stock option.

For example, if you believe that the stock price of a company that is currently trading for $ 100 will increase to $ 120 at a future date, you would buy a call option at a strike price of less than $ 120 (ideally, the price of exercise is not more than $ 120) subtracted from it the cost of the option, so the option is still profitable at $ 120). If the stock rises above the strike price, your option is money.

Similarly, if you think the company's share price will drop to $ 80, you will buy a put option (which entitles you to sell shares) with a strike price greater than $ 80 (ideally, a strike price of at least $ 80). plus the cost of the option, so that the possibility remains profitable at $ 80). If the stock falls below the strike price, your choice is money.

4. Determine the period for the option

Each option contract has an expiry period that indicates the last day that you can exercise the option. Here, too, you can't pick an appointment out of anywhere. Your options are limited to those shown when calling up a series of options.

There are two types of options, American and European, which differ according to when the options contract can be exercised. US Option holders can exercise at any time up to the expiration date, while European Option holders can exercise only on the day of expiration. Because US options offer greater flexibility to the option buyer (and more risk to the option seller), they generally cost more than their European counterparts.

Expiration dates can vary from days to months or years. Daily and weekly options tend to be the riskiest and are intended for experienced options traders. For long-term investors, monthly and yearly expiration dates are preferred. Longer maturities give stocks more time to move in and time to develop their investment thesis. As such, the longer the validity period, the more expensive the option.

What Is Day Trading And How Does It Work

A longer expiry is also beneficial because an option can hold its time value, even if the stock is trading below its strike price. The value of an option declines over time as expiration approaches; option buyers do not want to see their purchased options fall in value. They are likely to expire without value if the stock expires below the strike price. If the trade is against them, they can still usually sell the remaining time value of the option, which is more likely if the option is held longer.

WHAT IS THE STOCK MARKET?

The stock market refers to the public markets for the issuance, purchase, and sale of shares listed on a stock exchange or the over-the-counter market. Stocks, also known as stocks, represent partial ownership of the company, and a stock market is a place where investors can buy and sell these investable assets. A well-functioning stock market is critical to economic development, as it provides companies with the ability to access capital from the public quickly.

Stock Market Purposes

Capital income and investments in the stock market have two essential purposes. The first is to provide capital to companies that they can use to finance and expand their businesses. Suppose a company issues 1 million shares that initially sell at $ 10 a share. In that case, this provides the company with $ 10 million in the capital that it can use to grow its business (minus the fees the company pays an investment bank to administer the procedures). Show). By offering equity rather than borrowing capital needed for expansion, the company avoids incurring debt and paying interest on that debt.

The secondary purpose of the stock market

It is to provide investors, who buy shares, the opportunity to participate in the profits of publicly traded companies. Investors can benefit from buying shares in two ways. Some shares pay regular dividends (a certain amount of money per share).

Another way investors can benefit from buying shares is to sell their shares to profit if the share price rises relative to the purchase price. For example, if an investor buys shares in a company at $ 10 a share and the share price subsequently rises to $15 a share, the investor can make a 50% profit on his investment by selling his shares.

How Stocks Are Traded

stock exchanges and OTC are traded on exchanges such as the New York Stock Exchange (NYSE) or NASDAQ. Exchanges provide the market to facilitate the buying and selling of shares among investors. Exchanges are regulated by government agencies, such as the U.S. Securities and Exchange Commission (SEC), which oversee the market to protect investors from financial fraud and keep the exchange market running smoothly.

Although the vast majority of stocks are traded on exchanges, some stocks are traded over the counter (OTC), as buyers and sellers of stocks usually trade through a dealer or "market maker" who deals specifically with stocks. OTC stocks are stocks that do not meet the minimum price or any other requirements listed on exchanges.

OTC shares are not subject to the same public information regulations as listed shares, so it is not easy for investors to obtain reliable information about the companies that issue such shares. Stocks on the OTC market generally trade much less than publicly traded stocks, which means that investors often have to deal with large spreads between the bid and ask prices of OTC stocks. In contrast, stocks traded on an exchange are more liquid, with relatively small differences between supply and demand.

Fund managers or portfolio managers, including hedge fund managers, mutual fund managers, and ETF managers, are essential participants in the stock market because they buy and sell large amounts of stocks. Suppose a popular mutual fund decides to invest heavily in a particular stock. In that case, that demand for the stock alone is often significant enough to increase the price of the stock significantly.

Bullish And Bearish Markets And Short Selling

Two of the basic concepts of stock trading are "bull" and "bear" markets. The term bull market refers to a stock market in which the price of stocks is generally increasing. This is the type of market that most investors thrive in, as most investors in stocks are buyers, not short-sellers, of stocks. There is a bear market when stock prices are generally low.

Investors can still profit even in bear markets by short selling. Short selling is the practice of borrowing shares that an investor does not own from a brokerage firm that owns shares in a stock. The investor then sells the shares of the borrowed shares on the secondary market and receives money from the sale of that share.

If the stock price falls as the investor expects, then the investor can make a profit by buying enough shares to return the number of shares he borrowed from the broker at a lower total price than he obtained from selling the shares of the stock. Earlier at a lower price. Highest price.

For example, if an investor believes that Company A's stock is likely to fall from its current price of $ 20 per share, the investor can place what is known as a margin deposit to borrow 100 shares from his broker. He then sells those shares for $ 20 each, the current price, which gives him $ 2,000. If the shares later drop to $ 10 per share, the investor can buy 100 shares and return them to his broker for only $ 1,000, leaving him with a profit of $ 1,000.

How To Make Passive Money With Stocks?

The secret to making money from stocks? Keep investing for the long term, through thick and thin. Here's how to do it. The key to making money from stocks is to stay in the stock market; The amount of "time to market" is the best indicator of your overall performance. Unfortunately, investors often go in and out of stocks.

To make money investing in stocks, keep investing more time means more opportunities for your investment to grow. The best companies tend to increase their profits over time, and investors reward these higher profits with a higher share price. This higher price translates into a return for the investors who own the shares.

First things first. You'll need a brokerage account before you can start investing. Here's how to open an account - it only takes about 15 minutes.

Long time in the market also allows you to collect dividends if the company pays them. If you are trading in and out of the market daily, weekly, or monthly, you can say goodbye to those dividends because you probably won't own the stock at the critical points on the calendar to get the payout.

In other words, you would have earned twice the amount if you had stayed invested (and you don't have to watch the market either!) For just another critical ten days. However, no one can predict which days it will be, so investors must remain invested all the time to grab it.

Three Excuses That Keep You From Making Money With Investing

The stock market is the only market in which goods are sold, and everyone is afraid to buy. It may sound silly, but it is precisely what happens when the market is down even by a small percentage, as it often does. Investors are afraid and sell in a panic. However, when prices rise, investors jump straight in. It is a perfect recipe for "buy high and sell low."

To avoid these extremes, investors should understand the typical lies they tell themselves. Here are three of the biggest:

1. I will wait until the stock market is safe to invest in.
Investors use this excuse after a stock has fallen when they are afraid to buy in the market. Perhaps the stocks have been declining for a few days in a row, or maybe they have been in a prolonged slide. But when investors say they are waiting for it to be safe, they are waiting for prices to rise. So, expecting (perception) of security is just one way you end up

paying higher prices, and in fact, it is often just a perception of security that investors pay.

The motivation behind this behavior: Fear is a directed emotion, but psychologists call this behavior more specific "loss aversion due to myopia." That is, investors prefer to avoid short-term loss at any cost than to make a long-term profit. So, when you feel pain from losing money, you will likely do anything to stop that pain. Therefore, you either sell the shares or not buy even when the prices are low.

2. **I'll buy again next week when I'm lower.**

Potential buyers use this excuse while they wait for stocks to drop. research shows investors never know which direction the stocks will move on any given day, especially in the short term. A stock or market can rise just as easily as it drops down. Smart investors buy stocks when they are cheap and hold on to them over time.

The motivation for this behavior: can be fear or greed. A fearful investor may be worried that stocks will fall before next week and wait, while a greedy investor expects a drop but wants to try to get a much better price than the current one.

3. I'm tired of these stocks, so I'm selling them.

This excuse is used by investors who need a boost from their investment, such as working in a casino. But smart investing is boring. The best investors sit in their stocks for years and years, allowing them to multiply the profits. Investing is not usually a quick game. All earnings are held on hold, not while trading in and out of the market.

The motivation behind this behavior: the investor's desire for enthusiasm. This desire can fuel the delusional idea that successful investors trade every day for big profits. While some operators do it successfully, they focus hard and rationally on the result. It is not about emotions but about making money, so they avoid making emotional decisions.

HOW TO MAKE MONEY IN THE STOCK MARKET FOR BEGINNERS (STEP BY STEP PLAN)

Investing in the stock market has always been one of my favorite ways to grow my money. If you are a beginner looking for tips for making money in the stock market, here is a detailed step-by-step plan to start your investment journey. Before that, I want to share a story with you.

Recently, a friend asked me, "I want to invest in stocks. What stock is good to buy? He's a doctor and makes good profits, but he's never invested in stocks before. His original plan was to save enough money and buy more properties to earn rental income because his mother is an experienced realtor and advised him to put his money in real estate.

When he told me he wanted to invest in stocks, I was a little surprised, although I am not sure why you suddenly wanted to start investing in the stock market; this is not important at this point. The important thing is that you approach the stock market by investing in the wrong way. Why? Because you should not invest your hard-earned money in investments that you know nothing about. Of course, I haven't given him any stock recommendation.

This Is The Problem Of Buying Stocks Blindly On The Recommendation Or Advice Of A Friend.

Possibility 1: An action your friends recommend may be a success. However, the share price can fall and remain low for an extended period before finally rising. During this downtrend, are you content to hold stocks for a long-term profit? Since the only reason to buy the stock is that your friend thinks it's a good stock, you won't be able to stay calm in the face of mounting paper losses.

Possibility 2: The action your friends recommend could be a waste business. This is a genuine possibility because no one can predict where the share price will go in the future. If stocks are heading south, do you know and experience recognizing the warning signs of losing stocks?

Do You Also Have The Discipline To Cut Back On Your Losses?

Probably not. Because the only reason you invested in stocks in the first place is that your friend told you so. So instead of giving you stock advice, I suggest you get to know investing in stocks first.

The Basics Of Investing In Stocks

Now let's talk about some of the basics of investing in stocks. How does it work? The stock market is the grouping of buyers and sellers (a flexible network of economic transactions, not a separate physical entity or entity) of shares (also called stocks), representing ownership rights over companies.

So How Does The Stock Market Work?

Traders and investors buy and sell these shares based on how much they think the shares are worth or the direction the share price will go.

Four different ways to make money in the stock market

The first method: Buy low and sell high this is pretty clear. You buy a stock at a low price and sell it at a higher price for a good profit. It works the same way you buy products at wholesale prices and resell them for profit at a much higher retail price. If you have a firm belief that the stock price will increase over time, you can buy it now and then sell it when the price rises to the purchase price.

Method 2: sell short at a high price and buy back at a low price; you can also make money by shorting the stock at a high price and then repurchasing it at a lower price. When selling stocks short, you must first borrow the stocks before you can sell them short. This is a regulatory requirement.

There is an exception if you are trading intraday; you do not need to borrow the shares because you will repurchase them before the market closes. Note: Regulatory requirements regarding short-selling vary from country to country; therefore, you will have to check it and make sure that you comply with it.

Method 3: Earn Stock Income

There is a group of stocks called dividend stocks in the stock market. The parent companies of these dividend stocks pay dividends to shareholders once or twice a year, depending on the dividend schedule. Examples of dividend stocks include Coca-Cola Co, Philip Morris International, and IBM.

Method 4: put options on stocks

Options are a contract in which the option contract seller agrees to buy/sell the underlying shares at a previously agreed price (i.e., the exercise price) on an expiration date previously approved by the option contract buyer. When you sell stock options, you charge premiums to the option buyers.

A Step-By-Step Plan To Make Money In The Stock Market

The first step: understanding your investment objectives

First, you must understand your investment objectives. What are the objectives you want to achieve with your investments in the Stock Market? Do you want to increase the value of capital in the long term? Or do you want to earn constant income from your investment earnings every year?

Or are you interested in short-term investment earnings (i.e., trading stocks for short-term yields)? Or are you looking for monthly investment income? You need to define your investment objective because you will be able to find an investment strategy that can help you get the results you want.

For example, suppose you are investing for retirement and looking to raise capital for the long term. In that case, you will have a completely different investment strategy than anyone who just wants to trade stocks for quick capital gains in the short term.

The Second Step: Learn the basics of investing in the stock market now you have defined your investment objectives. What you need to do next is learn the basics of investing in the stock market.

Step 3: choose an investment strategy that suits your objectives and your risk profile; there are many different investment strategies you can choose from.

Here is a list of popular investment strategies:
- Value investment strategy

- Earning Growth Investment Strategy
- Passive investment strategy
- Invest in high-growth stocks
- Selective trade

Suppose you want to achieve steady dividend income from your equity investments year after year. Based on this, the best investment strategy for you would be a dividend investment strategy.

Dividend growth investment strategy involves investing in a company's shares according to future dividend forecasts. Firms that pay steady, predictable dividends tend to have less volatile stock prices. By investing specifically in dividend growth companies, you will be able to build a portfolio of dividend stocks that pay steady dividends year after year.

One of the best passive investing strategies is to invest the money in your retirement accounts in low-cost S&P ETFs (yes, even Warren Buffet recommends this).

On the other hand, if you are a seasoned investor and wish to select individual stocks and build a portfolio of stocks based on your analysis, then a value investing strategy may be more suitable for you.

Finally, if your goal is to trade stocks for quick capital gains based on technical analysis in the immediate term (for example, within a few minutes or a few hours), you would buy and sell stocks quickly and take advantage of the price action during market hours.

You will use a daily trading strategy to help you do this. The daily trading strategy is generally based on technical analysis (i.e., reading price charts). It uses price movements or patterns to predict how the stock price will move in the next few minutes or hours.

Fourth step: Create an investment portfolio with your investment strategy chosen; it is time to build your investment portfolio. First, I would like to introduce you to two concepts:

- Investment portfolio
- Diversification

An investment portfolio is a group of financial assets that an investor owns, including stocks, bonds, real estate, or alternative investments.

Diversification

means that you spread your money across different types of investments with little or no relationship. Why do you want to diversify your investments? Because you don't want to put all your eggs in one basket, and diversification can help reduce your investment risk. The correct way to invest your money is to build a diversified investment portfolio.

Let Me Give You An Analogy.

When you were young, you were told that to be healthy and strong; you had to eat a balanced meal that included cereals, dairy products, meats, vegetables, and fruits. Each type of food has its unique benefits for your body. Together, they give your body all the nutrition it needs.

But if you eat only one type of food or avoid one type of food altogether, your health is likely to suffer in the long term. You also need a balanced investment portfolio to reap the benefits of different types of market conditions and protect yourself from various adverse market conditions.

For example, when inflation is higher than expected, your investments in real estate and gold will perform better than other investments. When economic growth is worse than expected, your treasuries will perform better than other investments.

Therefore, you should always avoid investing all your money in one investment category. Instead, you need to create a diversified investment portfolio that matches your tolerance for risk and your investment objective. Of all the investment asset classes, stocks, real estate, and alternative investments are the riskiest, while investment-grade bonds are the least volatile and safest. Therefore, if you are a risk-averse investor, you may want to allocate more of your portfolio to bonds. However, if you are comfortable taking higher risks, you may want to issue more stocks.

Now, How Do You Build Your Portfolio?

Here are some questions to help you through the process of building your portfolio: How many stocks do you want to include in your portfolio? What are the sectors from which these actions come? What is the weight given to each sector or each share in your portfolio?

When you build your portfolio, you don't want to have just one share in your entire portfolio or just shares in a specific sector. Why? Because doing so will give you a high risk of concentration. To avoid high concentration risk, the key is to have a diversified portfolio. Likewise, having a lot of stocks is not good either.

Because it will not help improve the performance of your portfolio, one hundred different stocks will give you average returns that match the performance of the stock market index. In comparison, 15-20 well-handpicked stocks may give you exceptional returns. When it comes to building a portfolio, you must always strike a balance between return and risk if you do not want to create your investment portfolio.

Fifth step: risk management

One of the most important aspects of investing is money and risk management. Without reasonable risk and money management, you definitely won't be successful in investing. So what is good money and risk management? Good risk management means that you must always determine the maximum risk you are exposed to at the individual equity level, sector level, and portfolio level. For example, your entire investment account is $ 20,000. The maximum risk you are willing to take on an individual level is 5% of your complete account. If your loss is about to exceed 5%, you will reduce the loss. Many people end up losing a lot of money because they don't cut losses when they should.

Step 6: Review your portfolio

Once you create your portfolio, your work is not finished yet. You still need to review your portfolio periodically. Sometimes, some stocks in your portfolio can rise dramatically, while others don't move much or may decline.

You may encounter a situation where your exposure to a specific stock or group of stocks is very high in such cases. You need to rebalance the portfolio by reducing your holding in this particular stock or this particular group of shares and increasing your holdings proportionally in other stocks. Another reason you should reassess your portfolio regularly is that your investment objectives may change over time. When this happens, your current portfolio may not be suitable.

The Best Investment Strategies For Beginner Investors

Recommended Resources to help you make money on the Stock Market; therefore, to make money from the stock market, you must first know what good stocks you can invest in. However, no one can thoroughly scan the stock market for good investment opportunities because they just don't have the time. (By the way, there are roughly 4,000 stocks listed on US stock exchanges alone.) Plus, there are always other people who are more knowledgeable and experienced in a particular industry than you, so you're likely to miss out on some great stock ideas that are difficult to figure out on your own.

Making money on the stock market is not as easy as some people think. But it is not difficult either. If you have the right mindset, the right strategy, and the proper risk management, you should be able to see good results.

Easy Ways To Make Money On The Stock Market

Invest in what you know

Ideally, you should trade stocks that relate to what you know. For example, if you are a pharmacist, you should consider trading with pharmaceutical companies. If you are making a living from fishing, you should consider trading stocks related to fishing.

If you are investing in what you know, you may be a winner, as you may already have insight into stocks and know how well the companies behind them are performing. Consider reinvesting your winnings to make money in the stock market. Suppose you are a store owner and want your business to be more successful. One way to increase your profits is to reinvest some of it in the stock market.

However, you must ensure that not all of your winnings are used up, as there is always the possibility of losing money. Reduce your risk by investing only in what you can afford to lose. If you play it safe, you are less likely to leave feeling bruised.

How much you invest is entirely up to you, and it will depend on how much money you make each month. Try not to invest more than 10-15% of your profits and use the rest to boost your business in other ways.

You should also avoid placing more of your earnings on the stock market, even if you have gained 50% of your shares. It may seem worth risking more money at the time, but the prices can change quickly, so keep your money safe, and you won't regret it later.

Avoid High-Risk Stocks

If you are new to trading, you may be forgiven for risk. You may be tempted to risk a lot or all of your money on a few stocks in the hope that your risk is worth it, but you may be ready for failure. Let's imagine that the shares of a particular company increased three months ago by a whopping 75% and that each shareholder received a considerable sum. This business may see another increase in its share price, but again, that may not.

Don't bet that stocks will go up massively just because they have risen in the past; although they may rise again, you are unlikely to see another dizzying rally anytime soon.

Avoid high-risk stocks, especially if it appears that prices can go either way. Playing safe is the best way to preserve your money and reduce the possibility of loss. Exchanges also provide access to low-risk assets such as ETFs, options, and trading indices.

You can make money in the stock market, but you must be careful and invest your money wisely. Take your time, invest in what you know, reinvest your profits and avoid high risk. Take your time, be reasonable, and you can make a good profit.

How to go public with little money

You might think that investing and trading the stock market requires an injection of millions of dollars to make money.

This is simply not the case. Fortunately, we live in an age where almost anyone can start trading the stock market, and even if you don't have a lot of money to invest initially, there are a few ways to start trading.

Stocks are shares of a company. A small fraction allows you to own a small amount of a public company. You can earn money through dividends and trades where your stock values rise (or lose if they fall). There are many different trading strategies, even for those who don't have a lot of money to start with.

It's easy to assume that you can't own a share in a company for a small amount of money, but some stocks are affordable, and "partial shares" allow people to buy a portion of the stock rather than the whole thing.

Why is trading money less challenging?

So why would you need a different approach if you're looking to get started and don't have a lot of money? Why isn't it like investing in a great fund? Trading small numbers means you don't have the same buffer. Simply put, people planning to invest large amounts of money can mitigate these mistakes and even swallow some losses to get started and continue trading or wait for stocks to rally. Also, trading in small quantities is somewhat liberating, and the risks are possibly less. There are a few strategies you can follow when trading small amounts to try to get ahead.

Trade with leverage

Trading with leverage means that you can use options or collateral markets. These are leveraged markets that only require you to provide around 15% of the trade value in cash. If you were to trade individual stocks and shares directly, you might have to pay 30% of the cash value upfront. Sure enough, you can play in a bigger league than you could if you weren't using leverage. This should be something that you learn and fully understand before you begin.

Don't risk too much (unless you're prepared to lose)

When investing, it is usually a good idea to avoid risky stocks. You can assume that if you start with less money, this is free to take risks, and this is true for some investors who want to pursue this high-risk (potentially high-return) strategy.

If you take big risks and it doesn't pay off, you may lose your initial capital. In some cases, you can even lose it completely, so it is not just about losing a few percentages. If you need to protect the money you invest in and intend to increase it, even gradually and incrementally, you should adopt a risk aversion strategy. Traders with smaller starting accounts should calculate the risk/reward ratio they are happy with.

One piece of advice that many people stick to is the one percent risk rule. It gives you the same kind of buffer you would have if you were trading more significant amounts, but you need to be patient.

Use a trading account designed for lower amounts

There is no point in pretending that you are transferring large sums of money if you are not. So it is a good idea to know which trading platforms can allow you to trade with low amounts and not worry about commissions. Some offer minimal commissions, and others promise that there will be no commissions until your account reaches a specific cash value.

Also, it is a good idea to have a trading account that has an app and allows you to track your investments and make changes online.

Employer-sponsored retirement plans

This is probably the place to start if you haven't already. It's a little different than trading and investing on your own, as you don't have to choose where the money goes.

However, there are retirement plans available that can come in handy for tax reasons as well, making them an absolute no-brainer if you're looking to invest a little money each month. You can start with a 1% contribution, and you probably won't notice it every month. Also, tax deduction can make this more financially beneficial.

You won't see the benefits for several years, but this is usually a small price to pay, and having a retirement plan is always a good idea. This hands-off approach is popular with many people. If you wish, you can contribute more money to the fund so that you have more to benefit from in the future.

Use a monthly savings and investment fund

If you don't have a large amount of money to invest upfront, why not specify how much you can put into a plan each month and invest it in a mutual fund? Mutual funds are another area of the industry that technological advances have revolutionized. These funds are managed by third parties and come with different levels of risk associated with them.

You can choose to invest in a mutual fund, and you can invest more in the fund each month. This is equivalent to a financial advisor putting your money in a specific fund so that you do not have to make decisions on your own. Even if you don't have a lot of money to put in the box, monthly savings can be a great way to build your portfolio over time. If you are investing in a good fund, the interest compounded over months and years can start to rise. If you can start early, this puts you in a better position for the future.

Investing in little money is always a good idea, but the earlier you start in life, the greater the possibility of accruing compound interest.

There Are Several Different Strategies For Making Money From Investing In Stock

The truth is that it is a good idea to start in the way that seems best to you. You'll learn more about investing when you start than you learn from just reading. You can even use "fake" accounts with imaginary amounts of money so you can fully understand investing and know how to choose the right stocks, rather than risking your own money from the start.

Trading the stock market can be without intervention or with convenient training, depending on the type of commitment you want, or you can simply invest in a mutual fund or employer-sponsored plan to raise money for the future.

Returns From Trading Smaller-Volume Shares

Trading low-volume stocks can be hazardous. However, at high stakes, there can also be great rewards. In this book, we will discuss strategies for trading low-volume stocks and possibly profit-taking.

Lower volume stocks typically have an average daily volume of 1,000 shares or less. It may be owned by small, little-known companies listed on OTC exchanges but can also be traded on major exchanges. These stocks remain out of the mainstream of traders and investors and lack a general commercial interest. These stocks can be risky because their low volume leads to a lack of liquidity and facilitates price manipulation.

Smaller and newer companies are also disproportionately represented in smaller volume stocks. These companies can simply leave investors with nothing. Before you go into smaller-volume stocks, decide on your approach. Are you interested in short-term business profit, or are you investing long-term in an unfamiliar company you believe in?

Short-term traders can quickly profit from sporadic lower-volume stock price movements. Because very few stocks are generally traded, it doesn't take much to change the price of a stock drastically. However, there is always the risk that you may not be able to buy or sell stocks for maximum profit due to a lack of liquidity in inventory.

Long-term investors in low-volume stocks should be adept at evaluating a company's business prospects search, like these actions, and understand the company before investing. Experienced traders know that many little-known companies often go public on OTC exchanges to raise money, but only a few of them are successful in the long run.

Factors To Consider When Venturing Into Low-Volume Stocks:

1. Individual Profile - In stocks that trade sparingly where there are few or no market makers, consider assuming the role of the market maker. The market maker selects one stock (or two) and offers to buy and sell those shares by quoting the bid and ask price. It facilitates buying and selling to maintain liquidity.

In this role, a trader can take advantage of the lower liquidity by making a comprehensive offer, requesting spreads to the trading parties, and bringing in the difference. However, make sure you have a backup plan. Take a more limited stance instead of piling up a vast inventory that you might not be able to empty.

2. Macroeconomic factors: Trading in low-volume stocks could result from local or global macroeconomic factors. A country may go through a slowdown or recession as interest rates and inflation rise. These periods tend to be low in stock market activity. Shares that traded marginally before the recession are worse. But recessions and slowdowns always slow or subside long enough. Seasoned investors can use the extra capital to invest in specific winners who will reap high returns in the long run.

3. Take advantage of the general market rally: As the saying goes, "When markets go up, everyone makes money." The general market rise may be the result of government stability, falling oil prices, and other national or world events. In situations like this broad market rally, smaller-volume stocks are often the most advantageous.

DAY TRADING STRATEGIES FOR BEGINNERS

Day trading is the process of buying and selling a financial instrument on the same day or even multiple times throughout the day. Taking advantage of small price movements can be a lucrative game if played correctly. But it can be a dangerous game for a beginner or anyone who doesn't adhere to a well-thought-out strategy. However, not all brokers are suitable for the high volume of trades that day traders are making.

General Principles Of Day Trading

• Intraday trading is only profitable when traders take the matter seriously and do their research.

Day trading is a business, not a hobby. Treat it like this - be diligent, focused, objective, and alienate feelings from it.

• Here are some essential tips and knowledge to help you become a successful day trader.

Day Trading Strategies

1. Knowledge is power

In addition to knowing basic trading procedures, day traders should keep up with the latest news and events from the stock market affecting stocks - the federal interest rate plans, the economic outlook, etc. So do your homework. Make a list of the stocks you want to trade and stay informed of the selected companies and public markets. Browse trade news and visit trusted financial sites.

2. Putting money aside

Evaluate how much capital you are willing to risk on each trade. Many successful day traders risk as little as 1% to 2% of their account per trade. If you have a trading account of $ 40,000 and are willing to risk 0.5% of your capital on each transaction, the maximum loss per trade is $ 200 (0.5% * $ 40,000). Set aside an excessive amount of money that you can trade with, and prepare to lose it. Remember, it may or may not happen.

3. Make time, too

Day trading takes time. This is why it is called day trading. You will have to forgo most of your day. Don't even think about it if you have limited free time. The process requires the operator to keep track of the markets and discover opportunities that can arise at any time during business hours. Moving quickly is the key.

4. Start small

As a beginner, focus on a maximum of one or two actions during the session. Tracking and finding opportunities is more straightforward with just a few actions. Recently, it has become increasingly popular to be able to trade fractional stocks, so you can specify smaller specific dollar amounts that you would like to invest. This means that if Apple's stock is trading at $ 250 and you only want to buy $ 50 worth, many brokers will now allow you to buy a fifth of the stock.

5. Avoid the penny

You are most likely looking for bargains and low prices but stay away from smaller stocks. These stocks are often illiquid, and the jackpot chances are often daunting. Many stocks that trade below $ 5 a share are delisted from major exchanges and can only be traded over the counter (OTC). Unless you see a real opportunity and do your research, stay away from them.

6. Time for those occupations

Many orders placed by investors and traders start to take effect as soon as the markets open in the morning, contributing to price volatility. An experienced player can recognize patterns and make an appropriate decision to generate profits. But for starters, it might be better to read the market without making any moves for the first 15-20 minutes.

The averaging hours are usually less volatile; then, the movement begins to rise again towards the closing bell. Although rush hours offer opportunities, it is safe for beginners to avoid them at first.

7. Reduce losses with limit orders

Determine the type of orders you will use to enter and exit trades. Will you use market orders or limit orders? When you place an order in the market, it is placed at the best price available at that time, so there is no price guarantee. Meanwhile, the limit order guarantees the price, not the execution.

Limit orders help you trade more accurately by setting your price (not unrealistic, but executable) for both buying and selling. More sophisticated and experienced intraday traders can also use options strategies to hedge their positions.

8. Be realistic about earnings

The strategy does not need to win all the time to be profitable. Many traders only earn 50% to 60% from their trades. However, they get more from the winners than from the losers. Ensure that the risks in each trade are limited to a certain percentage of the account and that the entry and exit methods are defined and written.

9. keep calm

There are times when the stock markets test your nerves. As a day trader, you must learn to maintain greed, hope, and fear. Decisions should be governed by logic, not emotion.

10. Stick to the plan

Successful traders must move quickly, but they don't have to think fast. Why? Because they developed a trading strategy in advance, along with the discipline to adhere to this strategy. It is essential to follow your formula closely rather than trying to go for profit. Do not let your emotions control you and abandon your strategy. There is a mantra among day traders: "Plan your trade and trade your plan."

Basic Intraday Trading Strategies

Once you master a few techniques, develop your trading techniques, and define your ultimate goals, you can use several strategies to assist yourself in your pursuit of profit. Here are some popular methods that you can use.

• **Follow the trend:** Anyone who follows the trend will buy when prices are rising or falling when prices are falling. This is done on the assumption that prices that have been steadily rising or falling will continue to do so.

• **Adverse investment:** This strategy assumes that the rise in prices will reverse and decrease. The opposite is buying during the fall or short during the rally, with an explicit expectation that the trend will change.

Scalping: This is a technique in which the speculator takes advantage of small price gaps resulting from the spread of supply and demand. This technique usually involves getting in and out of a situation quickly, in minutes or even seconds.

• **News trading:** Investors who use this strategy will buy when good news is announced or short when there is bad news. This can lead to higher volatility, which can lead to increased profits or losses.

Day trading is challenging to master. It takes time, skill, and discipline. Many try to fail, but the techniques and tips outlined above can help you create a profitable strategy. With enough practice and continuous performance appraisal, you can significantly improve your chances of overcoming the odds.

Relative Strength Index

The Relative Strength Index is commonly used to determine the difference between the movement of a stock and the indicator and determine levels of overbought or oversold. Research shows that this is a mechanical interpretation that, judging by its strength, texts define their own overbought and oversold condition.

Traders need to be careful before making a decision based on the relative strength index. Most of the time, the stock will continue to rally support by solid momentum depending on the news or other fundamental reasons. The opposite is true when market momentum is weak. You will find many stocks in the oversold region due to the widespread sell-off.

Traders must differentiate between the correct oversold / overbought levels as defined by the behavior of individual stocks. Traders can also look for chart patterns on the RSI chart. The bearish pattern on the price chart may be accompanied by a negative divergence in the overbought region on the RSI chart, which serves as a kind of self-confirmation of an imminent decline.

If the RSI approaches the 70 marks and the stock price follows the same trend, there is always the possibility of a trend reversal from that level, and we may see some correction in action. Usually, the RSI should be studied in conjunction with other moving averages and other momentum indicators.

"If there is a sell signal on the RSI chart, it is necessary to seek confirmation from other technical indicators to improve the success rate in trading. Only when other indicators point to a downtrend, the trade should start in that direction."

RULES FOR SUCCESSFUL TRADING

- Always use an action plan
- Treat trade like a business
- Use of technology
- Protect your business capital
- Market study
- Risk only what you can afford
- Developing a work methodology
- Always use a stop-loss order
- Know when to stop trading
- Keep trading in the proper perspective

Each of the following rules is important, but when you work together, the effects are powerful. Taking it into account can significantly increase your chances of success in the markets.

Basic tips

- Deal with trading as a business, not a hobby or a job.

- Learn everything about the business.

- Set realistic expectations for your business.

Rule 1: Always use a business plan

A business plan is a set of written rules that outline the merchant entry and exit criteria and money management for each purchase. With today's technology, it's easy to test a business idea before risking real money. This practice, known as backtesting, allows you to apply your trading idea using historical data and determine if it is applicable. Once the plan is in place and the backtest shows good results, the procedure can be used for actual operations.

Sometimes your business plan doesn't work. Get out there and start over. The key here is to stick to the plan. Taking processes out of the business plan, even if it turns out to be a winner, is a bad strategy.

Rule 2: Treat business like a business

To be successful, you must treat trading as a full-time or part-time job, not as a hobby or a job. If it is treated as a hobby, there is no real commitment to learning. If it is a job, it can be frustrating because there is no regular paycheck. Trading is a business and incurs costs, losses, taxes, uncertainty, stress, and risks. As a merchant, you are primarily the owner of a small business and must research and strategize to maximize your business's potential.

Rule 3: Use technology to your advantage

Trading is a competitive business. It is safe to assume that the person sitting on the other side of the trade makes the most of all available technology. Charting platforms provide traders with an endless variety of ways to display and analyze the markets.

Testing the idea again with historical data avoids costly mistakes. Getting market updates through a smartphone allows us to monitor operations anywhere. The technology we take for granted, such as high-speed internet connection, can greatly increase business performance. Using technology to your advantage and keeping up with new products can be both fun and beneficial in commerce.

Rule 4: Protect your business capital

Providing enough money to fund a business account takes a lot of time and effort. It may be more difficult if you have to do this twice. It is important to note that protecting your trading capital is not synonymous with trying a losing trade. All traders have losing trades. Capital protection means not taking unnecessary risks and doing everything you can to maintain your business.

Rule 5: Be a market seeker

Think of it as continuing education; traders should stay focused on learning more every day. It is important to remember that understanding the markets and their intricacies is a continuous, lifelong process. Careful research allows traders to understand facts, such as the meaning of various economic reports. Focus and observation allow operators to hone their instincts and learn nuances.

Global politics, news events, economic trends, and even weather all impact the markets. The market environment is dynamic. The more traders understand the past and present markets, the better they are prepared for the future.

Rule 6: Only risk what you can afford to lose

Before you start using real money, make sure all of the money in this business account is expendable. If not, the merchant should keep saving until this is done. Funds in the business account should not be earmarked for children's college tuition fees or a mortgage payment.

Merchants should never allow themselves to believe that they are simply borrowing money from these other vital liabilities. Losing money is painful enough. It is even more so if it was the capital that should not have been risked in the first place.

Rule 7: Develop a fact-based methodology

It is worth taking the time to develop a solid trading methodology. It can be tempting to believe the "very easy" business gimmicks like printing money are spreading online. But facts, not feelings or hope, should inspire the development of an action plan.

Traders who are not in a hurry to learn to tend to have an easier time sifting through all the information available on the Internet. Keep this in mind: If you are going to start a new career, you will likely need to study at a university or University for at least one to two years before being eligible to apply for a position in the new field. Learning to trade requires at least the same amount of time and fact-based research and study.

Rule 8: Always use a stop-loss order

A stop loss is a predetermined amount of risk that a trader is willing to accept on each trade. The stop loss can be a dollar amount or percentage, but either way, it limits the trader's exposure while trading. Using a stop loss can take some of the trading pressure because we know that we will only lose an amount of X on a given trade.

Not having a stop loss is a terrible practice, even if it results in a profitable trade. Exiting with a stop loss, and therefore having a losing trade, is still a good trade if it conforms to the rules of a trading plan.

Ideally, you would exit all trades at a profit, but this is not realistic. Using a preventive stop loss helps ensure that losses and risks are minimized.

Rule 9: Know when to stop trading

There are two reasons to stop trading: an ineffective trading plan and an ineffective trader.

The ineffective trading plan shows much more significant losses than expected in the historical test; that happens, markets may have changed, or volatility may have decreased. For whatever reason, the business plan just doesn't work as expected.

Stay impassive and practical. It's time to re-evaluate your business plan, make some changes, or start over with a new business plan.

A failed business plan is a problem that must be solved. Not necessarily the end of the business.

An ineffective trader is someone who creates a trading plan but cannot follow it. External stress, bad habits, and lack of physical activity can contribute to this problem. A trader who is not in optimal trading conditions should consider taking a break. After dealing with difficulties and challenges, the trader can go back to work.

Rule 10: keep trading in perspective

Stay focused on the big picture when trading. The losing trade should come as no surprise; It is part of the trade. A profitable trade is just one step on the road to a profitable business.

Accumulated earnings make the difference. Once a trader accepts profits and losses as part of the business, emotions will have less impact on trading performance. This does not mean that we cannot be excited about a particularly profitable trade, but we must bear in mind that a losing trade is never far away.

Setting realistic goals is an essential part of keeping trading in perspective. Your business must achieve a reasonable return in a reasonable period. If you expect to be a millionaire by Tuesday, you are setting yourself up for failure.

Step Guide To Earning From Forex

These are the secrets of winning the Forex market that will allow you to master the complexities of the forex market. The Forex market is the largest in the world by value in dollars for average daily trade, making the stock and bond markets divided.

It provides traders with several inherent benefits, including the highest leverage available in any investment arena and the fact that there is movement in the market every trading day. There is seldom a day of trading in the forex markets where "nothing happens."

Currency trading is often hailed as the last big investment frontier. It is the only market in which a small investor with little trading capital can realistically expect to trade on his way to wealth. However, it is also the most traded market for large institutional investors, with billions of dollars in currency exchange worldwide every day as there is an open bank somewhere.

Currency trading is easy. It is difficult to trade well and make steady profits. To help you join the select few who regularly profit from forex trading, here are some secrets to winning in forex trading - five tips to help you make your trades more profitable and your trader's career more successful.

Step 1 To Winning Forex Trading - Pay Attention to Daily Pivot Points

Paying attention to daily pivot points is especially important if you are a day trader, but it is also important even if you are a focused trader, swing trader, or only trade in long-term time frames. Why? For the simple fact that thousands of other traders are noticing pivot levels.

Pivot trading is sometimes like a self-fulfilling prophecy. It means that markets often find support or resistance or make changes in the market at pivot levels simply because many traders will place orders at those levels because they are confirmed pivot traders. Therefore, when major trade moves occur outside the pivot levels, there is no fundamental reason for this move other than that many traders anticipated such a move.

It is not that pivot trading should be the sole foundation of your trading strategy; instead, regardless of your trading strategy, you need to monitor your daily pivot points for signs of trend continuation or potential market reversals. Look at the pivot points and the trading activity going on around you as a proven technical indicator that you can use in conjunction with whatever trading strategy you choose.

Step 2: Trade With An Advantage

The most successful traders are those who only risk their money when a market opportunity gives them an advantage, increasing the likelihood that the trade they initiate will be successful.

Your ledge can be any of several things, even something as simple as buying at a price level previously shown to provide significant support to the market (or selling at a price level that you identified as solid resistance).

You can increase your superiority and likelihood of success if you have several technical factors in your favour. For example, if a 10-period, 50-period, and 100-period moving average converge to the same price level, this should provide significant support or resistance to the market because you will get the shares of traders who base their trading on any of them. Moving averages work together.

A similar feature that converging technical indicators offer appears when the various indicators combine on multiple time frames to provide support or resistance. An example of this could be the price approaching the 50-period moving average on the 15-minute time frame at the same price level as it approaches the 10-period moving average on the hourly or 4-hour charts.

Another example of having multiple indicators in your favor is if the price reaches a specific support or resistance level, then the presence of price action at this level indicates a possible market reversal by forming a candle such as a Pin bar or a Doji.

Step 3: preserve your capital

In forex trading, avoiding significant losses is more important than making big profits. It may not sound perfect if you are a beginner in the market, but it is true nonetheless. Winning currency trading involves knowing how to preserve your capital.

Why is playing great defense, i.e., preserving your trading capital, so important in forex trading? The truth is that most of the people who try their hand at trading foreign exchange are unsuccessful because they are running out of money and cannot continue trading. They are taking advantage of your account before they even have a chance to enter what has turned out to be a very profitable business.

It is a slight exaggeration to say that having strict rules for managing risk and practicing it with sincerity almost guarantees that you will ultimately be a profitable trader. If you can only preserve your trading capital by avoiding crippling losses so that you can continue to trade, and ultimately a big winner, a "home run" trade, you will practically fall into your lap and drastically increase your profits and account size.

Even if you are a long way from being the "best trader in the world," your luck in the drawing, at the very least, will ultimately result in you stumbling upon a deal that makes more than enough profit for your year, or maybe even your entire trading career.

Step 4: Simplify Your Technical Analysis

Here are pictures of two very different Forex traders for you to consider:

Trader 1 has a large, luxurious desktop, a custom first-class trading computer, multiple displays, and market news feeds, and a ton of charts, all loaded with no less than eight or nine technical indicators - five or six moving averages, two or three momentum indicators, Fibonacci lines, etc.

The merchant 2 works in a relatively simple office space, using just a regular laptop or laptop. Examining its charts reveals only one or two, maybe three at most, of the technical indicators overlaid on the market price action. He might have been wrong if he guessed that Trader 1 was a very professional and successful Forex trader. The image of Trader 2 is similar to what the Forex Trader's trades would be like in that he constantly wins.

There are endless possible lines of technical analysis that a trader can apply to the chart. But more is not necessarily, or perhaps, better. Looking at an almost unlimited number of indicators generally only muddies the water for a trader, amplifying confusion, suspicion, and indecision, causing the trader to miss the forest for trees.

A relatively simple trading strategy, containing few trading rules and requiring compliance with minimum indicators, tends to work more effectively to produce successful trades. We know of a very successful Forex trader, a gentleman who takes money out of the market almost every trading day and has no overlapping technical indicators on the charts - no trend lines, no moving averages, no RSI, and certainly no RSI. without expert advisers. (EA) or trading robots.

Simple market analysis of it requires nothing more than a regular candlestick chart. Your trading strategy is to trade high probability candlestick patterns, such as pin bars (also known as hammer or shooting star patterns), which form at or near support and resistance price levels identified simply by observing the past price action in the market.

Step 5: Place your stop-loss orders at reasonable price levels

This truism may seem like only one element of preserving your trading capital in the event of a losing trade. It is, but it is also a key ingredient to winning in the forex market. Many novice traders make the mistake of believing that risk management means nothing more than placing stop-loss orders near your trading entry point.

Part of good money management indeed means that you should not trade stop loss levels too far from your entry point so that the trade gives an unfavorable risk/reward ratio (i.e., the risk is more in the event of losing the trade than you would reasonably do if the trade turned out to be the winner).

However, one factor that frequently contributes to unsuccessful trading is that stop orders are routinely executed near your entry point, as evidenced by a pause in trade at a loss, only to see later that the market turns in favour of trading and you have to bear it. Seeing the price rise to a level that would have returned you a considerable profit ... had a loss not stopped you.

Yes, it is only essential to enter into trades that allow you to place a stop loss close enough to the entry point to avoid suffering a heavy loss. But it is also vital to place stop orders at a reasonable price level, based on your market analysis. A basic rule often cited about placing a correct stop loss is that a stop-loss order should be placed slightly above the price that the market should not trade if your market analysis is accurate.

CONCLUSION

A successful trading practice does not guarantee that you will be successful when you start actual money trading. This is when emotions come in. But practicing successful trading gives the trader confidence in the system he uses if the system is generating positive results in a practice setting.

Deciding on a system is less important than acquiring enough skill to perform operations without hesitating or doubting the decision. Confidence is the key.

There is no way to guarantee that a trade will make a profit. The chances of a trader depend on his skill and win-lose system. There is no winning without losing. Professional traders know before they enter a trade that the odds are either in their favor or not. By allowing his profits to move and reducing losses, the trader could lose some fights but win the war. Most traders and investors do the opposite, so they don't earn consistently.

Traders who make consistent profits treat trading like a business. Although there is no guarantee that you will make money, having a plan is crucial if you want to be consistently successful and survive the trading game.

Trading low-volume stocks is a risky game. Potential returns are subject to many factors beyond the investor's control. An investor's best bet is to take a long-term perspective

Anyone looking to become a profitable stock trader just needs to spend a few minutes online to find phrases like Plan your deal and trade your plan and keep your losses to a minimum. For new traders, these stories may seem more of a distraction than practical advice. If you are new to the world of trading, you probably just want to know how to hurry up and make money

Understanding the importance of each of these business rules and how they work together can help a merchant build a viable business. Trading is hard work, and traders who have the discipline and patience to follow these rules can increase their chances of success in a highly competitive environment.

Like any other investment field, the Forex market has its unique characteristics. To trade profitably, a trader must learn these characteristics through time, practice, and study. Traders should pay attention to the helpful tips for winning in the forex market explained in this guide:

Pay attention to pivot levels

• Trade with an advantage

• Preserve your business capital

• Simplify your market analysis

- Place stopping points at truly reasonable levels

Of course, this is not all the trading wisdom you can get regarding the forex market, but it is an excellent start. If you consider these basic principles for winning in the forex market, you will have a clear trading advantage. We wish you all the best.

However, the bottom line is that his actual trading time is minimal every day, even if he is an active trader daily. The rest of the time, he must sit there, disciplined, waiting for the trade signals. When a trading signal appears, he should act without hesitation, following his trading plan.

Traders require discipline to do nothing when opportunities do not exist, but they must remain alert to potential opportunities. After that, they need the discipline to act in real-time when business opportunities arise. Once in a trade, traders must have the discipline to follow their trading plans.

CPSIA information can be obtained
at www.ICGtesting.com
Printed in the USA
LVHW080946281121
704655LV00002B/40